Jump Away

by James McGuire

illustrated by Larry Nolte

Printed in the United States of America

ISBN 0-15-317199-5 – Just a Jump Away

Ordering Options
ISBN 0-15-318586-4 (Package of 5)
ISBN 0-15-316985-0 (Grade 1 Package)

3 4 5 6 7 8 9 10 179 02 01 00

I am green.
I can jump very high.
Do you see me under
the rock?

What am I?

I’m a jumping frog!

I like to eat vegetables.
I can jump very high.
Have you found me under
the wall?

What am I?

I'm a jumping rabbit!

I came from far away.
I can jump very high.
Look! I am under the tree.

What am I?

I'm a jumping kangaroo!

Jumping is one way we have fun. Do you see us now?

Who are we?

We're like you!
We're just a jump away
from you.

Teacher/Family Member

Picture This!

Who was jumping in the story? Invite children to pantomime an animal that was jumping. Try to guess which one is being acted out.

School-Home Connection

Ask your child to read *Just a Jump Away* to you. Then have your child make up riddles about animals that jump.

Word Count:	94
Vocabulary Words:	green high under found came away way
Phonic Element:	Contraction: *'re* we're

TAKE-HOME BOOK

Bright Ideas

Use with "On the Way to the Pond" and "I Wonder."

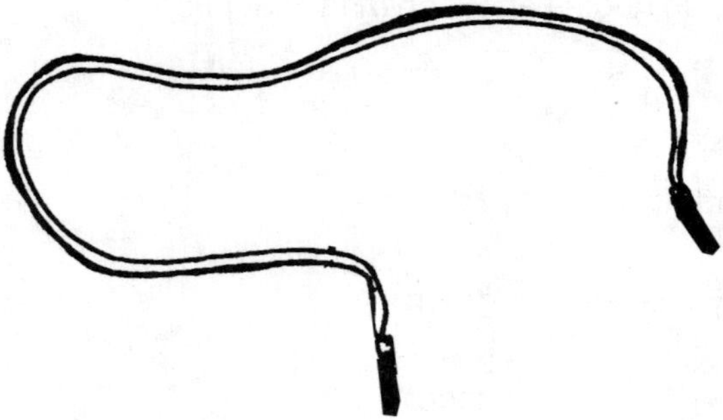